MEDITATIONS
for MUSICIANS

– o –

Midweek encouragement for Worship

Teams, Choirs and Instrumentalists

JOHN GAGE

John Gage Music
Siloam Springs, Arkansas

Nova Publishing
Bakersfield, California

Also by John Gage

"Brass Player's Warm Up and Practice Guide"
"Love, Dad"

Co Published by
John Gage Music
Siloam Springs, Arkansas
http://www.johngagemusic.com

Nova Publishing
Bakersfield, California
http://www.NovaPublishing.org
Nova Publishing and the "*NOVA*" logo are service marks belonging to
Nova Publishing, Bakersfield, California

FOREWARD

In some 42 years of full time music ministry, there have been many men and women of God who have shaped my ministry, my worldview, and my life. Here are four who have had a particularly significant impact:

My wife RUTHIE. Where I am weak she is strong, where I am clueless she is wise beyond her years. She has been loyal, forgiving, patient and courageous...THANK YOU Ruthie!

AUBREY EDWARDS, Minister of music at First Baptist Hendersonville, NC and Shades Mountain Baptist Church, Birmingham, AL. for many years. Aubrey taught me to dream big, to love people, and to have a deep desire to reach the lost. He rescued me on more than one occasion, when I wanted to bail out of ministry, and brought me groceries when my family was in great need.

GARY MATHENA, Minister of Music at Valley Baptist Church, Bakersfield, CA for 22 years. Gary has been a best friend, mentor, and co-laborer for some 20 years. Gary has taught me to see the future through God's eyes, and that faith is going to the edge of the light and taking one more step. He is one of the wisest men I have ever known, and has been both an encourager and a challenger to my Christian walk.

JOHN GLOVER, Minister of music at First Baptist Atlanta for over 30 years. John taught me the value of excellence, and attention to detail. He also taught me the value of transparency, integrity, and loyalty.

To these and many more I owe a deep debt of gratitude. None of us are in this alone....we all depend on those around us to teach us, guide us, encourage us and challenge us. I am very grateful for the men and women God has used in my life to shape my past and my future.

MEDITATIONS for MUSICIANS

INTRODUCTION

These devotionals are intended for worship ministry team members, and cover a wide variety of topics that are of interest to worship teams and instrumentalists.

There are 54 devotionals, organized in groups of four per month, with the final 4 available for months containing 5 rehearsal days. The devotionals do not have to be utilized consecutively, but can be used in any desired order.

The best use is to assign a devotional each week, and discuss that scripture and topic at rehearsal. These devotionals are not only designed as an encouragement and a challenge, but to provoke thought and prayer concerning YOUR particular worship team and ministry.

In the table of contents you will find the TOPIC of each devotional beside the title....You can select devotionals based on what your team needs or what is most appropriate at any given time.

Our prayer is that God will use these simple, heart felt devotionals to help strengthen your worship team, and to help develop a healthy perspective toward worship ministry. May God richly bless you in your continued service to Him.

John G Gage

www.johngagemusic.com

john@johngagemusic.com

MEDITATIONS for MUSICIANS

Midweek encouragement for Worship Teams, Choirs, and
Instrumentalists

TABLE OF CONTENTS

1 - THE THREE TYPES OF WORSHIP SONGS

"Let the message about the Messiah dwell richly among you, teaching

and admonishing one another in all wisdom, and singing psalms,

hymns, and spiritual songs..."

(Col. 3: 16 HCSB)

After 42 years of full time music ministry in Baptist churches, I am now "retired", at least from that particular ministry assignment, and now have an opportunity to visit other churches and to enjoy many various worship styles. This past Sunday I attended a "rock and roll" church...incredibly loud volume, worship leaders dancing as though the stage was made of hot coals, stage lights flashing wildly, choreographed lyrics on 3 huge screens. I didn't know ANY of the songs, so I watched the lyrics on the screen and worshipped in my heart as I read the words of each song...songs about God's great love, about grace and mercy, about our response to the Father's love through commitment and involvement, songs about God's Amazing Grace. And I worshipped. Until I wept.

Worship isn't about style...it is about CONTENT....Style is the wrapping paper and box....CONTENT is the gift within. If our spirits connect with scripturally accurate, thought-provoking, heart felt lyrics, then style (the wrapping paper) becomes insignificant.

The Apostle Paul encouraged the church at Colosse to worship using three distinct kinds of music:
- psalms
- hymns
- spiritual songs

The easiest way to describe the difference between these types of songs is this:
- psalms.....scripture ("Seek Ye First", "The Lord Is My Shepherd", etc)
- hymns....songs ABOUT God or directed TO God (A Mighty Fortress, Your Grace Is Enough)
- spiritual songs...testimony songs (Since Jesus Came Into My Heart, 10,000 Reasons)

Whether we sing in a choir/praise team, play an instrument in worship or participate in the congregation, our worship should be anchored to the *lyric*, rather than the style…give God the CONTENT, rather than the box in which it is presented.

THOUGHT: "Above all sing spiritually. Have an eye to God in every word you sing. Aim at pleasing him more than yourself, or any other creature. In order to do this attend strictly to the sense of what you sing, and see that your heart is not carried away with the sound, but offered to God continually; so shall your singing be such as the Lord will approve here, and reward you when he cometh in the clouds of heaven." (John Wesley)

2 - LIFTING UP HANDS

"Lift up your hands in the sanctuary and praise the Lord."

(Psalm 134:2 NIV)

My youngest grandchildren are 2 ½ and 16 months. Often the 2 ½ yr. old will face me, stretch out her little arms and say "Hold me, Gampa!" The younger one can't talk, but she will face me, lift her arms up and look longingly up at me...and I know EXACTLY what she wants! Nothing could thrill a grandpa more than seeing his grandchildren longing to be held. In Psalm 134 we have a very similar scenario...we are instructed to lift our hands to God as we worship.

Lifting hands to God does several things:

> 1) **It speaks of intimacy**. Often when I pick up my youngest she will pat my back... she just loves being close to "Gampa"...when we lift our hands to our heavenly Father we are expressing a desire to be close to Him... a desire to be held and to love Him back..

> 2) **It is an act of TRUST**. The act says" I know that you won't drop me...I know that I am safe up there!"

> 3) Spreading our arms to God **exposes our heart**. In effect we are saying, "I can't hide anything from You...I want you to take my emotions, my feelings, my deepest thoughts and desires, and use them for YOUR glory! I trust You with my innermost self!" Our Heavenly Father wants us to trust Him with our deepest thoughts, fears, joys, desires and emotional needs....He longs for us to be transparent with Him...He KNOWS anyway, but He wants His children to place their total trust in His divine ability to protect, provide and preserve.

Lifting arms to God doesn't HAVE to be a physical action, we can lift our hands in our hearts, but it doesn't hurt to actually go through the physical motions once in a while...especially in our private quiet time with Him. He loves to see His children stretch their arms up to Him!

THOUGHTS: "True faith, by a mighty effort of the will, fixes its gaze on our Divine Helper, and there finds it possible and wise to lose its fears. It is madness to say, "I will not be afraid;" it is wisdom and peace to say 'I will **trust** and not be afraid'." (Alexander McLaren)

3 - REBUKING THE ACCUSER

"Then he showed me Joshua the high priest standing before the Angel of the Lord, and Satan standing at his right hand to accuse him, and the Lord said to Satan, "the Lord rebuke you, Satan! Indeed the Lord who has chosen Jerusalem rebuke you! Is this not a brand plucked (rescued, delivered) from the fire?" (Zech. 3:1-2 HCSB)

I was young in the ministry and serving a small church. I was rather over-confident in my position as Minister of Music, and quite self-centered. One day the deacons called me in for a fateful meeting. I had been accused of saying and doing some hurtful and divisive things, and the deacons felt that my infraction was serious enough to warrant dismissal. I came home from that meeting a broken young man, convinced that God was finished with me and that my days of ministry were over. In the days that followed, Satan attacked, trying to convince me that I was finished. But God was lovingly moving behind the scenes, and soon opened another door which proved to be the pivotal step in moving me toward full time instrumental ministry.

In Zechariah 3, the high priest Joshua has been called on to assist in the rebuilding of the temple in Jerusalem following the Babylonian exile. Satan attacks him and accuses him before God of not being worthy of such a position of leadership, but God sternly rebukes Satan, saying "Is this not a brand plucked from the fire?" In other words, "Satan, I have rescued my servant Joshua from his failures and his past, and you are to leave him alone!!" What a relief and confidence-builder that must have been to Joshua! Then to validate that message, Joshua has his dirty cloths removed, and was clothed in "rich" or "royal" clothing!

God does that for us, too! When we accept Him as our own personal Savior, he removes the old garments and replaces them with His righteousness. Then when Satan accuses, God says "This one is MINE... leave them alone!!" Praise God today for His redeeming love!

THOUGHT: One cannot be found guilty of a crime for which the penalty has been "Paid in full."

"Jesus paid it all,
all to Him I owe.
Sin had left a crimson stain,
He washed it white as snow"

4 - A SMOOTH STONE

"Then he took his staff in his hand, chose five **smooth st**

the stream, put them in the pouch of his shepherd's bag an.., ...

sling in his hand, approached the Philistine." (I Samuel 17:40 NIV)

I carry in my pocket a smooth brown and white stone which I picked up on Moonstone Beach, close to Cambria, California. Every time I reach into my pocket to pull out change, I am reminded of what that stone went through in order to become smooth and shiny. If I had been that little rock, I would have said "OUCH!! The sand is hurting me! Stop rolling me around down here....it's PAINFUL!!"

Just like that little stone, God often has to apply the sandpaper of life to smooth out our rough edges, and to create the beauty in us that only He can see in our potential. That process is a painful one.

Often God uses people to polish us! Perhaps they are critical toward us, or maybe they ignore us. Sometimes they say hurtful things or speak unkindly about us to a friend. Our response to these times of polishing is very important. We need to react in love with kindness, even though we are hurting.

Often God uses circumstances to shape and mold us...John Peterson recounts the time he was passed over for a sure promotion...in his emotional pain he penned one of the most beloved hymns of all time: "No One Understands Like Jesus."

David chose SMOOTH STONES to fight Goliath. Do you know why? Smooth stones fly straighter, faster, and more accurately than rough ones. I want to be a smooth stone for Jesus, don't you? He can use me most effectively when He has shaped me just like He wants me to be!

THOUGHT: While being sanded to a smooth finish is painful, it is the only way to expose the inner beauty of that which is being polished.

5 - WE NEED EACH OTHER

"So then, we must pursue what promotes peace and what builds up

one another." (Romans 14:19 HCSB)

Just north of Kernville, California is a grove of Redwood Sequoia trees called The Trail of a Hundred Giants. These trees are mammoth examples of the variety and majesty of God's creation! They stand up to 300 feet tall, (that is a football field standing on end!!) and are so big around that a whole family holding hands cannot reach around the entire tree trunk.

Most trees have a tap root that extends deep into the ground, as far down as the tree is tall. But the Redwood Sequoia is different! The root systems to these gigantic trees go down three feet and then shoot straight out, just under the surface of the earth. The roots of one tree become entangled in the roots of its neighbor, and together they stand for centuries, supporting each other.

What can we learn from the giant redwoods? As we work closely with others, we should attempt to build one another up ALL the time. We should develop a YOU FIRST attitude, and we should attempt to always say and do that which is constructive and affirming, that which encourages the other person and helps them to be better equipped for the task to which God has called them. As we take the initiative to "promote peace" in this way, we will find ourselves leaning on each other, depending on each other and supporting one another, and the team will be strengthened as a result.

THOUGHT: If we don't stand together we can fall apart.

6 - NO GREATER LOVE

"Greater love has no one than this, that he lay down his life for his
friends." (John 15:13 NASB)

There is a story told of a young boy whose older brother was in a car
crash. The father approached the younger son shortly after the crash
and said, "Son, if you will, you older brother needs a blood transfusion
in order to live. The doctors have determined that only you can provide
this blood. Will you provide blood for your brother so that he may
live?" The younger son did not hesitate in answering he would indeed
help his older brother. Unknown to the little boy was the relative
simplicity and safety of the procedure.

The car ride to the hospital was unusually quiet for this normally very
talkative little boy. The father, at the same time in the most awkward
and difficult position of his entire life, thought best to leave the young
boy to his own thoughts. The father and young boy entered the now
familiar doors of the town hospital. As the father and son sat in the
hospital room, the nurse entered with the needle in hand. She
commented how courageous the young boy was, prepared the boys
right arm as she had done to hundreds of other patients over the years,
and slowly inserted the needle into his arm; the vial began to quickly
fill with the young boys blood. After the vial filled, the young boy, with
tears in his eyes, turned to his father and asked, "Daddy, how long do *I
now have* before I die?"

Much has been written about the 3 types of "love" in the Greek
language: brotherly love, romantic love, and God's unconditional
love...but to fully grasp the significance of the depth of love that led
Jesus to the cross is impossible. To think that the Word (John 1:1)
willingly suffered the most agonizing, deplorable death imaginable in
order to bring us into relationship with Jehovah God is beyond
comprehension. The words of this hymn by Frederick M Lehman just
begin to touch on this incredible love:

"Could we with ink the ocean fill, And were the skies of parchment
made, Were every stalk on earth a quill, And every man a scribe by

trade; To write the love of God above Would drain the ocean dry;
Nor could the scroll contain the whole, Though stretched from sky to
sky."

7 - SEASONED WITH GRACE

"Let your speech always be with grace, as though seasoned with salt,

so that you will know how you should respond to each person."

(Col. 4:6 NASB)

When I lived in Bakersfield, California, our home was 67 miles from a grove of Sequoia Redwood trees. I used to love to drive up into the mountains to stand in the shadow of these gigantic, strong trees. They grow to over 300 feet tall (a football field standing on end!!!) and live for hundreds of years. The Redwood has one unique feature which applies to the Christian walk. Their bark is soft and pliable, and can be pressed in several inches, but the inside of the tree is concrete solid, and virtually impervious to lightning, fire, disease and strong winds.

As we interact with people, and especially when we are tired or stressed, it is easy to become defensive, "short" in our verbal reactions, too sensitive in our response or hurtful to others. As we get to know our fellow team members better we can slip into unkind teasing, or even a verbally critical spirit. All of these things become hurtful and ultimately damaging to accomplishing our goal as worship leaders.

The story is told of a young lady who had said some very unkind things about a friend. She went to her pastor for advice, and he told her two things: That God and her friend could forgive her, and that she was to go to the top of the highest building in town, break a feather pillow and scatter the feathers over the street far below. Puzzled, she did as she was directed, and then went back to the pastor for further counsel. In the second session, he said "Now I want you to go back to the street beneath that building, and pick up every feather. "But", she exclaimed, "that is impossible!! They have blown everywhere by now!!" He replied "In the same way, while you can be forgiven, your words can never be retrieved, and can have a damaging impact from this day forward."

Let your speech be "with grace" today, "as though seasoned with salt", so that your testimony and the testimony of your team will remain un-compromised. Keep your "bark" or the part of you that interacts with others, soft and pliable, while your inner focus and purpose remains as solid and unchanging as steel.

THOUGHT: "Kind words can be short and easy to speak but their echoes are truly endless." (Mother Teresa)

8 - SPEEDBUMPS

But those who **wait on the Lord** Shall renew *their* strength

(Isa 40:31 NKJV)

I recently watched workmen install several speed bumps on the driveway outside my office window….that got me to thinking about speed bumps which GOD places in our lives! Several things are true of speed bumps:

- they are there to SLOW you down
- if you ignore them, you can do great damage
- they are there for YOUR protection and for the protection of others.

West coast theologian Dallas Willard, when asked about the key to a victorious Christian walk, replied "Ruthlessly eliminate hurry from your life." Often this is a difficult thing to do…and not necessarily because we want to make another dollar or buy another toy. Often our busyness has to do with ministry, and with a desire to be available to help others. As people involved in ministry we need to slow down now and then, sharpen our spiritual focus, rest our weary bodies, and gain a new perspective. When Elijah was feeling defeated after some great spiritual victories, God told him to rest….then woke him up and fed him, told him to rest again, and woke him up and fed him a second time, THEN Elijah continued his ministry. (I Kings 19)

Maybe God has placed some strategic speed bumps in your path to slow you down a bit…when you recognize a trial as a divine speed bump, PAY ATTENTION! If you ignore it, you can do great damage...to yourself, your family, your friends, your music group, your church. Sometimes the most spiritual thing you can do is slow down and rest….

THOUGHT: "In place of our exhaustion and spiritual fatigue, God will give us rest. All He asks is that we come to Him...that we spend a while thinking about Him, meditating on Him, talking to Him, listening in silence, occupying ourselves with Him - totally and thoroughly lost in the hiding place of His presence." (Chuck Swindoll)

9 - TRUSTING GOD FOR THE LITTLE THINGS

"My God will supply ALL you need according to His riches in glory
in Christ Jesus" (Phil. 4:19 NASB)

In late August of 1968, I flew (alone for the first time) from Baltimore to Tulsa, and from there was to meet up with Tulsa resident and high school friend Gail Caywood to be taken by her parents the additional 90 miles to Siloam Springs, Arkansas to begin my college career at John Brown University. When I arrived at the Tulsa airport I immediately went to a pay phone to call Gail so she could pick me up, but I couldn't find her phone number ANYWHERE! Finally I decided to look in the phone book, only to find three full pages of Caywoods! In my pocket I had 2 dimes, and a check with which I would buy my initial books and supplies for the new school year. Not knowing what else to do, I put my first dime in the phone and called the first Caywood in the book. These folks had never heard of Gail, John Brown, me or anyone else that I knew!! SO....I had a little prayer meeting! I put my last dime in the phone, and noticed that one of the Caywoods in the phone book was in bold type. Taking this as a positive sign, I dialed that number, Gail's dad answered, they picked me up at the airport, fed me lunch and carried me the final 90 miles of my journey.

Does God supply our every need? YES! Have you heard the song... "Why do I worry, why do I fret....He's never failed me yet"? It's true. What needs and concerns do you have today? "Take your burdens to the Lord and leave them there."

THOUGHT: "Trust in yourself and you are doomed to disappointment...but trust in GOD and you are never to be confounded in time or eternity." Dwight L. Moody

10 - APPOINTED FOR ALL THE SERVICE

"Their kinsmen the Levites were appointed for ALL the service of the tabernacle of the house of God." (I Chronicles 6:48 NASB)

After serving as minister of music in several churches for eight years, the Lord opened a door to serve a great church as their first full time Minister of Instrumental Music. I had been accustomed to planning worship and being on stage, but now I was learning to fill folders with the correct parts, set up rehearsal rooms and then re-set the room for a Sunday School class, edit parts and move percussion equipment.

One day, while setting up chairs in the worship center in preparation for the following Sunday, I became angry. I remember saying to myself, "I am better than this!!" I should be "writing some masterpiece" or ministering to somebody, rather than having to mess with these stupid chairs!!!" Suddenly the arrogance of my heart struck me, and I dropped to me knees in tears and asked God to forgive the prideful condition of my heart. That day God reminded me that my role was to be SERVANT, not master. I was to serve not only the people God had placed in my charge, but in serving them I was serving Jesus Christ!! I was reminded that day that God had "appointed me to ALL the service of the tabernacle", not just that which made me look good or allowed me to feel appreciated.

There's a great little verse tucked away in I Corinthians 10, v. 31 which says "Whatever you do, do ALL to the glory of God!" Sometimes it is good to be reminded that serving is not always glamorous or humanly rewarding. Sometimes our service will seem menial or unimportant. Often it will go unrewarded or even un-noticed! But in God's eyes it is all a "sacrifice of praise" as we serve faithfully and quietly, out of the spotlight. And one day, when we stand before the Father, we will receive the only reward that really counts: "Well done, My good and faithful servant."

THOUGHT - "The highest form of worship is the worship of unselfish **Christian service**." (Billy Graham)

11 - SECOND FIDDLE

"Do nothing out of rivalry or conceit, but in humility consider others as more important than yourselves...." (Phil. 2:3-Holman CSB)

On a choir mission trip to Israel we took two people who were confined to wheelchairs. What a joy to see choir folks assisting those who needed help with steps, needed help getting on or off the bus, who couldn't see the sights up close without assistance. I was amazed at the selflessness of so many of our choir members as they helped those who could not help themselves.

When Leonard Bernstein was asked which instrument he considered to be the most difficult, his response was "Second fiddle!!" We all have a built-in self-preservation mechanism that screams "ME FIRST!!" We feel that if we don't TAKE first place, we will never GET first place....but that is the exact opposite of God's economy!

In music ministry this concept is tested every week...who will get the solo?? In which chair will I be placed? Will I get to sing on the Praise Team this week?? Will I be standing on the front row, or the last row? Will I be beside that "uncomfortable" person, or by my best friend? Will we do the songs "I like" or will we do songs that seem boring or repetitive to me? In each of these scenarios and hundreds more, our initial thought should be, "How can I practice playing second fiddle today?"

In 2008 Sara Tucholsky was competing for the Great Northwest Athletic Conference softball championship. She blasted a homerun over the center field wall, and as she rounded second base she realized that she had failed to touch first...as she turned to go back to first and touch the bag, she felt excruciating pain in her knee. Falling to her face she tried to make it back to first, realizing that if a team mate helped her the run would be disqualified. It was at that point that two girls from the opposing team, Mallory Holtman and Liz Wallace, picked Sara up, and carried her around the bases, making sure that her left foot touched each base. Who have YOU helped to win today??

THOUGHT: "What does love look like? It has the hands to help others.

It has the feet to hasten to the poor and needy. It has eyes to see misery and want. It has the ears to hear the sighs and sorrows of men. That is what love looks like." (Augustine)

"Then Ezra blessed the Lord, the great God, and all the people

answered, AMEN, AMEN!! While lifting up their hands; then they

bowed low and worshipped the Lord with their faces to the ground"

(Neh. 8:6 NASB)

It would be a vast understatement to say that the church is divided by worship styles. Today's church is FRAGMENTED -offering various kinds of services to meet the needs of various demographic people groups, trying to please everyone stylistically while often losing sight of our true audience, our Heavenly father! There seem to be 3 schools of thought. Worship should be:

> UPWARD- with a sense of holiness and a "proper" liturgical approach to the Almighty,
> OUTWARD- with great celebration, joy, participation and exuberance
> INWARD- reflective, quiet, introspective and humble

In Nehemiah 8 we see all three perspectives simultaneously! There was an OUTWARD expression ("AMEN, AMEN!!"), an UPWARD expression ("while lifting their hands") and an INWARD expression ("they bowed low") as God's people worshipped Him.

When I was young my family loved to gather around the piano and sing hymns or carols together. Each of us had our favorites, and we sang them ALL during those times. As a church we need to remember that we are a family, and we need to appreciate various expressions of worship so that each family member will be able to communicate with God in their language.

THOUGHT: "Blessed are the balanced." Warren Wiersbe

13 - THE POWER OF PRAYER

"And Hezekiah prayed to the LORD: "LORD, the God of Israel,

enthroned between the cherubim, you alone are God over all the

kingdoms of the earth". (II Kings 19:15 NIV)

Earlier in I Kings we see Rabshakeh threatening Hezekiah and the Israelites. It was a serious threat, because the Assyrian army had been leveling everything in its path, and Israel was next in line! Hezekiah sends to the prophet Isaiah for some spiritual guidance, and Isaiah assures the king that God will intervene. But Rabshakeh the bully isn't through with his threats just yet. In verses 8-13 of II kings 19 he mocks the God of Israel, brags about the strength of the Assyrian army and threatens to annihilate Israel. This time Hezekiah does what he should have done in the first place: he goes to God in prayer.

Hezekiah's prayer is in 3 parts:
- He RECOGNIZES the power of God (v. 15)
- He RECOUNTS his nation's plight (vs. 16-18
- He REQUESTS deliverance (v. 19)

And in verse 35 God DOES defend Israel in answer to Hezekiah's prayer, and 185,000 of the enemy are miraculously slain, causing the frightened remnant to flee.

Have you seen the simple acrostic on HOW to pray? It looks like this:
- Adoration
- Confession
- Thanksgiving
- Supplication

It is a good formula to begin praying with **worship,** as Hezekiah did. Then in view of God's Holiness, **confession** comes more easily. That naturally leads to a season of **gratitude** for God's forgiveness, blessing, protection and provision, and that leads into a time of **making requests** on behalf of others and finally for ourselves. When confronted with the power of the Heavenly Father, the enemy HAS to flee!

THOUGHT: "The man who has heard from God has the enduring power to engage adversaries...and surmount any problem that lies in his path..." – Dr. Charles Stanley

14 - WAITING

"I waited patiently for the Lord, and He inclined to me and heard my cry." (Psalm 40:1 NKJV)

Noted author John Ortberg quotes Robert Levine's book "The Geography of Time" where Levine suggests the creation of a new unit of time called the HONKO SECOND, which he describes as being the amount of time between when the light changes and the person behind you begins honking his horn. We live in an impatient world….we want every problem solved in 27 minutes, the time it takes to watch a TV show, minus commercials!

God's timing is perfect! He is never early, never late. He knows when we need it NOW, when we need it LATER, and when we don't need it at all. Sometimes what we need the most is the development of an attitude of patience. Sometimes what we ask for would actually hurt us if God were to allow it, and His Divine protection answers "No".

Henri Nouwen writes of his friend the trapeze artist. The moment when the flyer lets go of the trapeze and hangs suspended in space must feel like an eternity. Nouwen's friend writes "The flyer must never try to catch the catcher. He must wait in absolute trust. The catcher will catch him. But he must wait. His job is not to flail about in anxiety. In fact, if he does it could kill him. His job is to be still, and wait. And to wait is the hardest work of all."

What are you waiting for today? While the Psalmist "waited patiently," God was there; listening, instructing, providing, and empathizing, all behind the scenes. He is there for you today as well….be patient.

THOUGHT: Never think that God's delays are God's denials. Hold on; hold fast; hold out! Patience is genius. (George-Louis Leclerc de Buffon)

15 - THE ULTIMATE DESTINATION

"For You, O God tested us. You refined us like silver. You brought us into prison and laid burdens on our backs. You let people ride over our heads. We went through fire and water, but you brought us to a place of abundance." (Psalm 66: 10-12 NIV)

In 1804, then President Thomas Jefferson selected 28 year old Merriweather Lewis and 32 year old William Clark to explore the westward flowing Missouri and Columbia rivers, to determine if passage could be made to the Pacific Ocean by this route.

Through the long, hot summer of 1804 they laboriously worked their way upriver. Numerous navigational hazards, including sunken trees, sand bars, collapsing river banks, and sudden squalls of high winds with drenching rains slowed their progress.

There were other problems, including disciplinary floggings, two desertions, a man dishonorably discharged for mutiny, the death of one of the team leaders, and hostile Indian bands. Imagine the exultation of this band of explorers when they crested the final bluffs, and saw the grandeur of the Pacific Ocean spread before them!!

Our spiritual journey is impeded by temporary setbacks. These could come in the form of discouragement, heartache, financial difficulty, family challenges, relational difficulties and spiritual dryness. We often face times of crisis with health, vocation and major decisions at key crossroads in our lives. God often uses these situations to test the strength of our faith. He wants us to see for ourselves just how much we depend on Him, and how much we become frustrated and discouraged by our circumstances. If we are patient, and if we endure the temporary setbacks with a sense of faith and dependence, God will bring us to "a place of abundance." Don't give up too soon!!

THOUGHT: The purest silver has been subjected to the most intense fire.

16 - BEARING MUCH FRUIT

"I am the vine, you are the branches; he who abides in Me and I in

him, he bears much fruit, for apart from Me you can do nothing".

(John 15:5 NASV)

Evangelist Leo Humprey was visiting with a Godly, elderly woman who was well known for her ministry as a prayer warrior. Leo asked her to pray that God would use him, and she responded "Don't pray that God will USE you, pray that God will make you USEABLE, and He'll wear you out!"

How are we useable to God? What makes an apple or a bunch of grapes juicy, tasty and desirable? If a fruit becomes detached from its vine, it withers and shrivels, becoming useless. If it remains in the vine, and is tenderly watered and pruned, it becomes a succulent, tasty and refreshing pleasure.

When I First went to a large church with an expansive television ministry, I was overwhelmed. I remember sitting in my office weeping, because I felt so unqualified and unprepared for this ministry assignment. As I prayed for guidance, I recall hearing a "still, small voice" speak to my heart and say, "Anything of significance which happens through your ministry here will not happen on the podium, but on your knees." God gently and lovingly reminded me that he was not nearly as concerned with my ability or experience as He was interested in my ABIDING, and receiving from HIS hand the strength, guidance and insights necessary for accomplishing a task which seemed impossible.

To ABIDE is to trust, to stay attached, to gain nourishment from, and to dwell. As you abide in Him, you will bear much fruit.

THOUGHT: The gardener is never closer to the branch than when He is pruning it.

17 - GOING THE EXTRA MILE

"Whoever forces you to go one mile, go with him two…therefore you

are to be perfect (mature), as your Heavenly Father is perfect

(mature)…" (Matthew 5: 41, 48 NASB)

In Jesus' day a Roman soldier could require that a Jewish boy accompany him for a mile to carry his heavy bags. In discussing loving ones' enemies, Jesus said, "If someone forces you to go one mile, go with him two…" WHY would Jesus suggest going above and beyond what was required, especially when one was being FORCED to carry a soldier's belongings? It has to do with TESTIMONY.

What would a soldier think, if after the required mile he commanded, "OK, drop the bags and get out of here!" only to have the Jewish lad respond "I'll be glad to help you for another mile if you like, Sir!" What would that say about the character, family and upbringing of the boy?

Singer Dave Boyer, after he accepted the Lord and went from singing in clubs to singing in churches, recounts the times he would arrive at a church early to rehearse with his accompanist, only to have the accompanist show up to late to rehearse for the service. He said on more than one occasion, "When I was singing for the world we would practice 4 hours a day and every weekend to make sure it was right, but now that I am singing for the King of Kings, I can't even get a piano player to show up 30 minutes early to rehearse!"

In Galatians 4:9, Paul puts it this way "Let us not lose heart in doing good, for in due time we will reap if we do not grow weary." Just what will we reap? Ministry done with excellence. A reputation for perseverance. And one day a commendation from the Savior, "Well done, my good and faithful servant."

THOUGHT: I don't know what your destiny will be, but one thing I know…the only ones among you who will be really happy….are those who will have sought and found how to serve." Albert Schweitzer

18 - SERVING WITH JOY

"Serve the Lord with gladness; Come before His presence **with** singing". (Ps 100:2 NKJV)

Have you ever had a bad weekend? Maybe some relational challenges, family problems, financial set- backs, health issues? Have you ever climbed out of bed on Sunday morning, wishing it was ANY day of the week other than SUNDAY?

In Ps 100:2 there are two complementary phrases, each with two parts:

- SERVE- the Lord with gladness

- COME BEFORE HIS PRESENCE with singing

Have you ever stopped to think that our WORSHIP is an act of SERVICE, an act of OBEDIENCE?

When we come together to lift up the name of Jesus, we are expressing our desire to bless HIM, to focus on HIM, to obediently accomplish the task to which HE has called us...there is no ME in our worship, only HIM.

As we sing and play, our hearts are filled with joy. As our hearts express joy, the natural overflow is expressing that joy in song...JOY and SINGING fit together perfectly...one leads to the other.

As we obediently serve with joy, our voices and instruments will express the attitude of our hearts through making music BEFORE Him, directed TO Him....and His great heart will be blessed.

THOUGHT: When you have no helpers, see your helpers in God. When you have many helpers, see God in all your helpers. When you have nothing but God, see all in God. When you have everything, see God in everything. Under all conditions, stay thy heart only on the Lord. – **Charles Spurgeon**

19 - STRENGTH OUT OF WEAKNESS

"And everyone who was in distress, everyone who was in debt, and

everyone who was discontented gathered to him. So he became

captain over them. And there were about 400 men with him. (I

Samuel 22:2 NKJV)

I remember hearing an evangelist talk about being born lame, and spending the first seven years of his life in leg braces. Later in life, long after his legs had regained normal strength, he was questioning God as to the purpose of this early disability. I recall hearing him say "God revealed to me that I would be working with the spiritually crippled all my life, and I needed to know what it felt like to be lame!"

This passage in I Samuel 22 recounts an all-time low in David's life. He lies to Ahimelech the priest, eats bread reserved for the priesthood, pretends to be insane in order to protect himself from the Philistine King Achish, and flees for his life, hiding in caves. In the midst of this, one beautiful example of the providence of God stands out. During this difficult time, all of the distressed, discontented debtors are drawn to David, and they become a faithful band of followers who go on to win incredible victories.

I Cor. 1:27-29 (NKJV) states "But God has chosen the foolish things of the world to put to shame the wise....and the weak things of the world to put to shame the things that are mighty...and the things which are despised God has chosen...that no flesh should glory in His presence."

In II Cor. 12:9 (NKJV), Paul states "And He (God) said to me, 'My grace is sufficient for you, for My strength is made perfect in weakness.'"

Are you weak today? Are fear and doubt beginning to crowd faith out of your life? Be grateful. For your very weakness opens the door for God to do great and mighty things in and through your life and ministry.

THOUGHT: "Not by might nor by power, but by My Spirit, says the

Lord" (Zech. 4:6 NASB)

20 - EXTRAVAGANT WORSHIP

"Mary then took a pound of very costly perfume of pure nard, and anointed the feet of Jesus and wiped His feet with her hair; and the house was filled with the fragrance of the perfume.

(John 12:3 NASB)

The story of Mary anointing the feet of Jesus is a powerful illustration of extravagant worship. In John 11, Mary's brother, Lazarus dies, and Jesus resurrects him from the grave. In the next chapter Mary is overwhelmed with gratitude and as an expression of her love and thankful heart she breaks open a bottle of very expensive perfume, and anoints the feet of Jesus. This was an act usually reserved for burial, when a box or jar of precious ointment would be broken, the deceased anointed with the fragrance, and then the pieces of the bottle would be buried with the body.

This bottle was filled with "spikenard", a rare perfume available only from India. It is very possible that Mary had saved for years to buy this bottle, and was saving it for her own burial.

This perfume was worth about one year's wages…when Mary gave to Jesus, she gave with incredible generosity and sacrifice.

Mary broke the box and gave ALL of the perfume to Jesus. She withheld nothing!
Here are the applications for us:

- We should give generously in worship
- We should give completely in worship
- We should give sacrificially in worship

THOUGHT: Jesus gave his best…His ALL for us. Our response should be to give our best; our all for Him in worship.

21 - DRIVING ON EMPTY

"Come unto me, all ye that labour and are heavy laden, and I will give you rest". (Matthew 11:28 KJV)

There have been very few times in my life when I have exerted a maximum amount of energy, but one experience I recall vividly! We had taken a pop-up camper to Colorado on vacation, and a brother-in-law thought it would be a great idea for us to take a hike in the mountains. We started off just fine, but the first 1,000 feet were straight up!! 11 miles and over 5 hours later we emerged from the forest exhausted, thirsty, and soaking wet (from the thunder storm we had hiked through!!)

There are times in our spiritual walk when we are exhausted spiritually, physically, emotionally and mentally. Sometimes it feels like we can't take another step. Occasionally it feels as though we have walked through a thunder storm miles from loved ones, and we are uncomfortable and homesick. God knows our condition!

Missionary Alfred Perna was ministering in a very poor part of Italy. When his duties were completed, he and his son began the 400 mile drive back to Rome, but realized that they only had enough money to buy 6 gallons of gas! They watched the gas gauge needle steadily drop until it almost reached empty, and then it froze. As they drove through Naples with the gas gauge registering almost empty they prayed and drove on. As they drove up to their apartment in Rome, the car sputtered and died, with the fuel tank empty.

God will do that for YOU!! When the emotional, physical fuel tank is almost empty, He will stretch your resources and help you make it all the way home! Keep your eyes on Him; the finish line is in sight!!

THOUGHT: "When you find He's all you have, you'll find He's all you need." (Gary Mathena)

22 - ENCOURAGEMENT THROUGH TEAMWORK

"Also with the lute I will praise You and Your faithfulness, Oh my God!! To You I will sing with the harp, O Holy One of Israel!"

(Ps.71:22 NKJV)

As a musician with a rather artistic temperament, I have a tendency to let little frustrations become big discouragements. I sometimes struggle with depression when faced with criticism or negativity. For several years I have kept an "appreciation file" of notes from folks who have graciously written to me, and when I begin to be overwhelmed by discouragement, I read a few notes from people who have been an encouragement. Here are a couple of excerpts from my file:

> "Dear John…the entire orchestra sounds so professional….the instrumental solo this past Sunday night was just awesome…."

> "Dear John….the orchestra sounded really GRRRRRREAT this past week! The orchestra and heralding trumpets added so much to the service…."

> "Dear John, after the orchestra played Sunday morning I could have left the service, having heard a fresh and meaningful word from the Lord… (P.S. Don't mention this note to my pastors!!!)"

We all need encouragement from time to time. Col. 3:16 says, "Let the word of Christ dwell in you richly, teaching and admonishing one another in all wisdom, singing psalms and hymns and spiritual songs, with thankfulness in your hearts to God." Music ministry can have a tremendous impact on the listener, and can be a tremendous encouragement to the participant. Music can and should be used to instruct, encourage and uplift. As you offer this important "sacrifice of praise", seek to encourage those around you.

THOUGHT: - "When I worship, I would rather my heart be without words than my words be without heart." Lamar Boschman

23 - ALL YOUR HEART

"But be sure to fear the LORD and serve him faithfully with all your

heart; consider what great things he has done for you."

(I Samuel 12: 24 NIV)

I remember hearing pastor Jack Hayford recount a mission trip story...he was visiting a remote tribe and when they worshiped they did a little dance.in his heart pastor Hayford said "Isn't that a foolish little dance! Why do they feel that they have to worship THAT way?" while having a quiet time back home he was trying to pray, and he felt like his prayers were being blocked...he prayed "Lord, why aren't you hearing me?" He heard God speak to his heart and say "If you want to have a clear channel of communication with me, I want you to dance before me like that tribe danced. At first reluctantly, and then with abandon, he danced that dance before the Lord, and suddenly felt his prayers breaking through."

We don't have the right to judge the way someone else worships....God speaks to different people in different ways...we DO need to make sure that we are worshipping with ALL OUR HEART, without judgmental spirits, with a spirit of "awe" before the master, and with pure motives and clean hearts. God longs for His children to worship Him, but if we are approaching our times of worship with arrogance, pride, or thinking that we worship correctly while others worship incorrectly, God will not hear us, and those times of worship will be ineffective and empty.

THOUGHT: "There is a difference between going to a service "for the worship" and going to a service "to worship the Lord." The distinction appears to be a minor one, but it may imply the difference between the worship of God and the worship of music! "(Sinclair B Ferguson)

"...since you know that you will receive an inheritance from the Lord as a **reward**. It is the Lord Christ you are serving".

(Col. 3:24 NIV)

In 2002 a team of 8 of us from Valley Baptist Church, Bakersfield, CA went to Pristina, Kosovo to hold a retreat for the missionary staff there and to encourage the small Baptist congregations in that Muslim country. Karen Watson, one of the team members, fell in love with the nationals there, and developed a tremendous passion for seeing those people accept Christ! Upon her return, she felt called into full time missionary service, made all of the necessary preparation, and began her service in the Middle East.

On March 15, 2004, Karen was shot to death in Iraq as she and her companions searched for locations from which to offer humanitarian aid to the Iraqi people. A small and deeply saddened group of us met at the Bakersfield airport to escort Karen's body to the funeral home, and I was privileged to play "Amazing Grace" at the graveside as her body was laid to rest. At her memorial service, Pastor Phil Neighbors read a letter Karen had left the pastoral staff, to be opened only in the event of her death. Karen had penned these words:

"I wasn't called to a place
I was called to Him,
to obey was my objective, to suffer was expected
His glory my reward
His glory my reward"

Karen was right! We aren't necessarily called to a PLACE, we are called to HIM! To bring glory to Him no matter where we are should be our primary goal. As the apostle Paul put it, "...it is the Lord Christ you are serving..."

THOUGHT: "To obey was my objective, to suffer was expected, His glory my reward...

25 - I AM DOING A GREAT WORK AND CANNOT COME DOWN

"Sanballat and Geshem sent a message to me, saying, Come and let us meet together in one of the villages in the plain of Ono. But they were planning to harm me. So I sent messengers to them, saying, "I am doing a great work and I cannot come down. Why should the work stop while I leave it and come down to you?"

(Neh. 6: 2-3 NASB)

Andy Stanley, in his book "VISIONEERING" teaches lessons on leadership gleaned from the book of Nehemiah. One of the important principals of leadership has to do with dealing with obstacles that interfere with accomplishing our goals.

In Nehemiah 6, 3 adversaries are trying to distract Nehemiah from his goal of completing the walls around Jerusalem, and they devise a plan to put him out of commission....permanently. But Nehemiah sees through their devious plan, and refuses to be distracted from the task God had assigned for him.

In this story we see 3 possible obstacles to accomplishing our goals:

> OPPORTUNITIES- we should always sacrifice the GOOD for the sake of the BEST, and that requires deep discernment. Often possible opportunities are really distractions in disguise.

> CRITICISM- If God has called us to a task, then criticism should be ignored. Sometimes criticism can be helpful....especially in refining our methodology, but often it is just hurtful and distracting, and can be discarded.

> FEAR- there is no reason to be crippled by fear when God has called us to accomplish a task.

Andy recounts the story of a friend of his who was given a unique opportunity for a coveted acting job. As she evaluated the opportunity, she realized that it would interfere with her duties as "Mom", so she turned it down. A few weeks later, on Mother's Day, her daughter gave her a hand-made card. On the first page was a hand reaching down, and underneath were the words "I am doing a great work"…the next page showed a small hand reaching up, with the words "And cannot come down." What are your priorities today? YOU ARE DOING A GREAT WORK…….

"Consider it a great joy, my brothers, whenever you experience various trials, knowing that the testing of your faith produces endurance." (James 1:2, 3 HCSB)

The book "The Heavenly Man" is about A Chinese pastor who suffered immeasurable torture and imprisonment for his faith. After 13 years of nearly unbearable persecution, he was freed and was ushered out of the country and into Europe. While in the care of his new European friends, they told him "We are praying for the deliverance of the church in China". His response was truly incredible, and is indicative of what he learned about faith while imprisoned. He replied, "Pray not for lighter burdens, but for stronger backs!"

Are you under fire today? Are there trials in your life situation that seem overwhelming? God promises to give us "grace to help in time of need" as we approach His throne with boldness.

In order to build strength, a weight-lifter adds weight, which in turn adds resistance. As he presses against the added resistance, his muscles become stronger. Don't fight the trials in your life today. Allow God to make you stronger by providing some "Divine resistance". Even while you are pressing against the added weight, He is helping to ease the burden and make you more like He wants you to be.

He Giveth More Grace

He giveth more grace as our burdens grow greater,

He sendeth more strength as our labors increase,

To added afflictions He addeth His mercy,

To multiplied trials he multiplies peace.

27 - LEAVING YOUR WATER POT

"So the woman left her water pot, and went into the city, and said to
the men, 'Come, see a man who told me all the things that I have
done. This is not the Christ, Is it?'"   (Jn. 4:28-29 NASB)

Fruitland Baptist Bible Institute in Hendersonville, NC exists to train
men who feel called to full time ministry later in life. Many of these
men have left positions as executives of major corporations or their own
businesses in order to follow God in preparation for pastoring a church.
While serving as minister of music in nearby Etowah, NC, I had the
privilege on several occasions of leading worship for their weekly
chapel services. WOW can these guys ever sing!! They are thrilled to
be headed into full time ministry in obedience, and I never heard ONE
of them complaining about giving up the income or prestige that came
with the positions they had left behind.

In the familiar Bible story of the encounter between Jesus and the
woman at the well, a small phrase often escapes our notice. "She left
her water pot." That was why she had come to the well in the first
place...to draw water!! When confronted by the giver of "living water"
she suddenly had a new set of priorities, and her original intent seemed
insignificant. She had met the omniscient, compassionate Christ, and
her life was changed forever!

Maybe you have a "water pot" you need to leave behind today, in order
to obediently follow Christ. Perhaps there is a friendship which has
been a distraction, or maybe a career goal has kept you from serving
God effectively. Perhaps a hobby or similar activity has become too
important and is taking too much time. Whatever it is, there is
incredible joy in leaving the water pot behind in order to follow Jesus.

THOUGHT: It is always wise to trade a clay water pot for the jewel of
an obedient life.

28 - PRESSING ON

"I **press** toward the mark for the prize of the high calling of God in Christ Jesus." (Phil. 3:14 KJV)

When my grandfather passed away on Jan. 8, 1962, my grandmother wrote this poem:

"Home at last, the life's long journey ended!

The pilgrim's feet now tread the golden shore.

And he beholds the face of Christ His Savior,

and is at home with Him forevermore…

And so we travel on toward that glad morning

when we shall meet our loved one once again

Where there will never be another parting,

and with the Lord forever we shall reign!" (Marion Gerow)

A missionary returned to the U.S. from many years of faithful service in Africa. On the same ship was a US dignitary of great fame. As the ship approached New York harbor, the statesman was welcomed with great fanfare, bands, speeches and celebration, but there was no one there to meet the missionary. As he settled into his humble and sparse room for the night, He began to pray, "Lord, why was there no one there to meet me when I came home?" It was then that He heard the Father gently say, "But my child, you aren't home yet."

As we "press on", and there are obstacles, challenges, and thankless days and nights of service to the King, remember that you aren't home yet! There will be a prize, a reward, for those who faithfully serve Him, but for now the prospect of hearing "Well done, my good and faithful servant" is enough.

THOUGHT: Earthly rewards pale in significance when compared to eternal rewards.

29 - TO WILL ONE THING

"But if any of you lacks wisdom, let him ask of God and it will be given to him. But he must ask in faith, without any doubting, for the one who doubts is like the surf of the sea, driven and tossed by the wind. For that man ought not to expect that he will receive anything from the Lord, being a double-minded man, unstable in all his ways."

(James 1:5-8 NASB)

This passage from James 1 discusses a common challenge among believers- the ability to be genuine...to WALK the TALK. Once a person places his trust in Jesus for forgiveness of sin and the beginning of a new life, there oftentimes remain old habits, desires, activities and thoughts which need to be brought under the control and Lordship of Christ. James instructs us to ASK for what we need, without doubting.

The great philosopher Soren Kierkegaard put it this way, **"Purity of heart is to will one thing."** What are we "willing" for? Do we try to present a GOD side to family and fellow worshippers, while retaining a ME side around co-workers? Are there things in our lives that we feel we need to hide from our fellow-worshippers? If so, we are "double-minded." How do we overcome this malady? Fact is, we can't! Yes, we can discipline ourselves to a degree to behave in a certain way, but only God can change our "wills" and make us willing to be molded into His shape. Paul nestled 3 little words in a chapter on living authentic Christian lives. Right in the middle of I Thess. 5 he said "Pray without ceasing."

What does that look like? It means keeping the vertical lines of communication open. It means maintaining an attitude that recognizes the closeness of Jesus every minute of every day, in every activity and every thought. It means that the road to spiritual maturity is paved with trials and temptations, and every victory is another brick on the road to living a life that is pleasing to God. James sums it up this way: "Blessed is a man who perseveres under trial; for once he has been approved, he will receive the crown of life which the Lord has promised to those who love Him." (James 1:12)

What are we willing to give up, in order to be used by Jesus in the greatest possible way?

THOUGHT: "The best place any Christian can ever be is to be totally destitute and totally dependent on God, and know it." (Alan Redpath)

30 - WALKING ON WATER

"And He said "Come!". And Peter got out of the boat, and walked on

the water and came toward Jesus" (Matt. 14:29 NASB)

Have you ever been asked to do something which was seemingly impossible? When I first went to First Baptist Atlanta as Minister of Instrumental Music, I was overwhelmed by the task. The musicianship of many of the orchestra members was far better than mine. I was surrounded by what seemed like spiritual giants, and I felt like a spiritual pygmy in comparison! The television ministry was huge and imposing, and I felt a lot of pressure to build "perfection" into the orchestra. For the first three weeks of my tenure there I sat at my desk and wept every day, and "told God" that He had chosen the wrong person for the job!! As I began to listen to His "still, small voice" I heard this, "Anything of lasting value in this ministry will not be accomplished on the podium, but on your knees!"

I love the story of Peter walking on the water. It was around 3 AM when the disciples looked through the high waves that battered their small craft and saw what appeared to be a ghost. As soon as Jesus said "Take courage! It is I; do not be afraid", Peter put his faith to the test by asking if he could meet Jesus half way. We criticize Peter for taking his eyes off of Jesus and placing them on the storm, BUT HE WAS THE ONLY ONE WHO GOT OUT OF THE BOAT!!!

God may be asking you to "get out of the boat" today. Maybe the task to which He has called you seems overwhelming. Perhaps you don't feel qualified. There may be circumstances in your life which cause you to momentarily take your eyes off of Jesus and look at the storm around you. As soon as Peter cried out in fear, Jesus stretched out His hand and lifted Him up! Trust Him to do the same for you! He will never call you to a task for which He is not preparing you! "Take courage!...Do not be afraid!"...Go ahead and step out of the boat!!

THOUGHT: "God doesn't call the qualified, He qualifies the called."

31 - THE COST OF WORSHIP

"A woman came having an alabaster flask of very costly oil of
spikenard. Then she broke the flask and poured it on His head."

(Mark 14:3 NKJV)

Missionary Jim Elliot was murdered by the Auca Indian tribe of Central
Ecuador in 1956. The day before his death, he had written in his diary,
"He is no fool who gives what he cannot keep to gain what he cannot
lose." Material possessions are transitory at best; giving our lives and
resources as an act of worship is an *investment*, rather than an
expenditure.

Worship is always accompanied by sacrifice. In our **witness** we
sacrifice the potential of alienation from friends and comfort zone. In
our **service** we sacrifice our time and abilities. In our **giving** worship
begins after the tithe has been met and our hearts have been moved to
go beyond that which is required as an expression of love. Experts tell
us that the ointment used to anoint Jesus in today's passage was worth
at least a year's wages! This woman's act of worship cost her
something.

Scott Wesley Brown's song HE IS NO FOOL was inspired by Jim
Elliot's life and martyrdom:

I've lost track of all the Sundays the offering plate's gone by

And as I gave my hard-earned dollars I felt free to keep my life.

I talk about commitment and the need to count the cost,

But the words of a martyr show me

I don't really know His cross.

Obedience and servant-hood are traits I've rarely shown

And the fellowship of His sufferings is a joy I've barely known.

There are riches in surrendering that can't be gained for free

God will share all Heaven's wonders

But the price he asks is me.

THOUGHT: Our problem is that we worship our work, work at our play, and play at our worship." -Gordon Dahl

32 - WHAT WE GIVE GOD HE BLESSES

"He replied, "YOU give them something to eat. ...He said to His disciples, "Have them sit in groups of about 50 each.....Taking the 5 loaves and 2 fish and looking up to heaven, He gave thanks and broke them. Then He gave them to His DISCIPLES to distribute.... they all ate and were satisfied, and the disciples picked up 12 basketfuls of broken pieces that were left over." (Luke 9: 13-17 NIV)

We are all familiar with this story, but I want to point out a couple of things that pertain to music ministry.

1) Jesus said "YOU give them something to eat" (v.13)...they thought they were there to listen, learn, take in, but Jesus was interested in their SERVICE....in their putting into action what they had already learned! And that is why you are in worship leadership. He has called you to serve, and you have been obedient to that call.

2) When they gave the lunch to Jesus, HE BLESSED IT (v.16) here is the principle...**WHAT WE GIVE TO JESUS, HE BLESSES.** That could be your abilities, your time, your finances, your family...whatever it is, when our resources are given to God, He blesses them.

3) He BROKE them, and GAVE THEM TO HIS DISCIPLES to distribute. (v.16) Here is the principle...**WHAT GOD GIVES TO US, HE MULTIPLIES.** After Jesus had blessed the lunch, He BROKE it....and gave the pieces to His disciples to distribute, and there was more than enough. As God gives us our abilities, resources, relationships, knowledge, whatever it may be, He multiplies those things for HIS glory and for the spiritual nourishment of His family.

4) What God blesses and multiplies is always enough (v.17). Why do you think the disciples took up 12 baskets of leftovers? Because 12 of them distributed what Jesus had given them...it

was a lesson in "enough". Do you ever feel that you aren't talented enough, smart enough, old enough, gifted enough, capable enough…when God gives you ANYTHING, it is enough.

THANK YOU for allowing God to use you as ministers….He has called you, he has blessed you and has blessed what you have brought to Him to use, and He is multiplying your ministry for His glory!

33 - MAKING MUSIC JOYFULLY

"Sing to Him a new song; Play skillfully with a shout of joy."

(Ps. 33:3 NASB)

Charles Kettering once said "People are very open-minded about new things, as long as they're exactly like the old ones." It is a fact....we are reluctant to change....someone has said "The only difference between a rut and a grave is the dimensions." If we keep doing the same old things over and over, our expressions of worship become so routine they lose all effectiveness....it is like hearing a person pray the exact same prayer for 30 years....we wonder if that person EVER has a fresh experience with the Heavenly Father!!!

In Ps 33:3 we are instructed to sing a **NEW** song...that means we discover and share a *fresh* expression of God's grace, His character, His mercy, His patience, His power, His creativity, His faithfulness. The word "new" is the exact same word that is used in Lamentations 3:22-23..."for His compassions never fail, they are NEW every morning: great is your faithfulness" (NIV). Because God's mercies are new, our expressions of worship should be fresh, imaginative, and new.

In Ps 33:3 there are three phrases we should note:

- NEW song

- play SKILLFULLY

- SHOUT of joy

In addition to worshipping with a fresh, new expression, our worship leadership should be done with **excellence**. God deserves our VERY best, and that requires personal preparation, skill development, study of texts and lyrics, musical preparation and group preparation. There is no shortcut to singing or playing with excellence. It takes work.

Finally our worship should be with abandoned joy. When we realize the extent of Jesus' sacrifice for us, and the relationship with God that is possible as a result of that sacrifice, how can we help but worship, sing and play with 100% of our attention, our engagement, our focus and our involvement? As we develop our skills, and seek fresh, meaningful expressions of worship, our hearts will be filled with the deepest gratitude imaginable, which will overflow in joyful song.

THOUGHT: If a man just stops to think what he has to praise God for, he will find there is enough to keep him singing praises for a week. (D.L .Moody)

"When the priests came forth from the holy place (for all the priests who were present had sanctified themselves, without regard to divisions), and all the Levitical singers, Asaph, Heman, Jeduthun, and their sons and kinsmen, clothed in fine linen, with cymbals, harps and lyres, standing east of the altar, and with them one hundred and twenty priests blowing trumpets in unison when the trumpeters and the singers were to make themselves heard with one voice to praise and to glorify the Lord, and when they lifted up their voice accompanied by trumpets and cymbals and instruments of music, and when they praised the Lord *saying*, "*He* indeed is good for His lovingkindness is everlasting," then the house, the house of the Lord, was filled with a cloud, so that the priests could not stand to minister because of the cloud, for the glory of the Lord filled the house of God.

(II Chron. 5: 11-14 NASB)

This Scripture is rather lengthy, but we need to extract some principals from the dedication of Solomon's temple that apply to worship today.

- **The worship participants were spiritually prepared**. They had ALL been to the "holy place", a place of spiritual cleansing and prayerful preparation.
- **They played and sang in unison....with one voice-** not only were their HEARTS prepared, but their RELATIONSHIPS were prepared
- **They sang about the goodness of God-** Notice that their song never once used the words "me" or "my" or "I"....they focused on HIM
- **God showed up in unbelievable glory-** When our hearts are spiritually in tune with God and in unity with our fellow-worshippers, and we focus on GOD'S character and

HIS activity in our lives, it opens a pathway to God's presence in our gatherings.

THOUGHT: Fruitful and acceptable worship begins before it begins. (Alexander MacLaren)

35 - SHARING HOPE

"I wait for the Lord, my whole being waits, and in his word I put my **hope**". (Psalm 130:5 NIV)

I have a friend who is serving his 5th year of a 10 year prison sentence. He is in his 60's, non-violent, and has a degenerative nerve disease, he has lost his family, his home and his career ...I have communicated with him consistently over the past 5 years, and as his disease worsened, I felt led to hire an attorney to appeal the length of his sentence. The judge vacated a very large restitution demand, but would not reduce the length of the sentence...so I hired an attorney to file for clemency, and the governor of that state is considering that appeal now. Recently I received this note from my friend:

> "Thank you again for your very active, real friendship. When I am so close to total despair and defeat, just losing all hope, I think of all you've invested in me and our friendship, and I realize I MUST survive to honor that."

You and I have a unique privilege in music ministry....we share a wonderful message of HOPE. We have no idea what people in our churches are facing every Sunday: rebellious teenagers, financial ruin, relational challenges and heartache, difficult work circumstances or even job loss, family or personal illness, religious persecution...the list is endless. Every congregational package, every praise team/choir/orchestra song points to a powerful, loving Heavenly Father and offers hope to a hopeless world...and hope to a church that is facing increasing turmoil and adversity. It is a privilege to share HOPE through music ministry!!

THOUGHT: The presence of hope in the invincible sovereignty of God drives out fear. (John Piper)

36 - HOW BIG IS GOD?

"You alone are the Lord. You made the **heavens**, even the highest **heavens**, and all their starry host, the earth and all that is on it, the seas and all that is in them. You give life to everything, and the multitudes of heaven worship you". (Neh. 9:6 NIV)

Our Milky Way galaxy contains some 100 Billion stars, and is 100,000 light years from end to end. Astronomers tell us that our galaxy is one of over 100 BILLION galaxies, each containing between 300-500 BILLION stars. Scientists used to believe that a specific area of space was a black hole, until the Hubble telescope revealed 3,000 GALAXIES in that area!! One star, in the Canis Major galaxy is called VY Canis Majoris, and it is so huge that if our earth were the size of a golf ball, and you filled the state of Texas to a depth of 22 inches with them, they would ALL fit inside this one star!

Gen. 2:1 states "Thus the **heavens** and the earth were completed in all their vast array." Psalm 19:1 says "The **heavens** declare the glory of God; the skies proclaim the work of his hands." It is impossible for finite minds to grasp the power, the creativity, the awesome majesty of our Creator, but science gives us a small taste of His greatness!

Country artist Ray Price says it this way:

> "Though men may strive to go beyond the reach of space
> To walk beyond the distant glimmering stars.
> This world's a room so small within my Father's house
> The open sky but a portion of his yard.
> How big is God? How big and wide is his vast domain?
> To try to tell these lips can only start;
> He's big enough to rule the mighty universe,
> Yet small enough to live within my heart."

"Do not conform to the pattern **of** this world, but be transformed by
the renewing **of** your mind. Then you **will** be able to test and approve
what **God**'s **will** is—his good, pleasing and perfect **will**".
(Rom. 12:2 NIV)

The island of Inagua in the Bahamas is known for their export of salt.
Huge ships dock there, are loaded with salt, and export it all over the
world. The harbor channel is very narrow, so Inagua harbor built 3 tall
poles on the dock, one after the other…when the ship captain lines up
the bow of the ship where he can only see the first pole, he knows he is
in the center of the channel and can dock safely.

God's will is like that…there are 3 "markers" we can use to determine
God's will for our lives:
- God's Word (His moral will)
- The ministry of the Holy Spirit to our hearts (His permissive will)
- The advice and counsel of Christian leaders, friends and pastors

When we allow these three markers to adjust our thinking, we can be
fairly confident that we are headed in to the safety of the channel of
God's will for our lives. God doesn't want His will for us to be a secret,
but often the process of "seeking" is a valuable tool for the child of
God.

My wife Ruth and I were facing a life-changing, ministry- altering
decision…we didn't want to make the wrong choice because our future
as a family rested on making the right decision. We PRAYED about it,
we searched God's word for guidance according to Scriptural
principals, and I called my dad and two dear pastor friends for their
counsel. After weighing these 3 "markers", we made the decision, and
the result was a change in ministry location that altered our lives and
ministry for the next 20 years. Trust His Word, and the voice of the
Holy Spirit in your hearts, consult with Godly counsel, and allow God
to "change your thinking" so you will discover His very BEST for you.

THOUGHT: "To walk out of His will is to walk into nowhere." (C.S. Lewis)

38 - THE SONG OF MOSES

"I will sing to the Lord, for he is highly exalted. Both horse and driver he has hurled into the sea. The Lord is my strength and my defense; he has become my salvation." (Ex. 15: 1a, 2a NIV)

In addition to the full version of this song in Ex. 15, The Song of Moses is also mentioned in Deut. 31, Deut. 32 and Rev 15. At the end of Ex 15 Moses' sister Miriam grabs a tambourine and reprises the first portion of this song again. Psalm 66: 10-12 reprises a portion of this song as well...evidently it was a very important song to the children of Israel.

The song of Moses is a hymn of praise for God's deliverance from the armies of Pharoah, and holds a great pattern for our worship.

- Praise God for **WHO HE IS**. In vs. 2, 3, God is praised for many of His attributes, and for His powerful name. It is always a good idea to begin worship with remembering who God is.

- Praise God for **WHAT HE HAS DONE**. From v. 4-11 God is praised for the miraculous delivery from Pharoahs armies...His power, His salvation, His victory. It is always a good idea to praise God for what He has done.

- Praise God for **WHAT HE IS GOING TO DO**. Vs. 11-17 Moses proclaims future victories with faith and confidence...once we see and remember what God has done, we can face the unknown without fear.

Moses ends His song by singing "The Lord reigns forever and ever!" If you are moving through a challenging time today, remember WHO God is, recall past victories, and face the future with confidence that God will make a way. He is the same yesterday, today and forever! (Heb. 13:8)

THOUGHT:" The greatest faith is born in the hour of despair. When we can see no hope and no way out, then faith rises and brings the victory." Lee Roberson

39 - The RIGHT HAND OF GOD

"For I am the Lord your God who takes hold of your right hand and says to you, Do not fear; I will help you. (Isa 41:13 NIV)

Think about this…if we are walking with God, and he holds us by our right hand, then he is holding us with HIS LEFT hand, which leaves HIS right hand to act on our behalf! God's Word has a LOT to say about the significance of God's right hand:

- In Ex. 15 His Right Hand destroys the enemy
- In Ps. 16:11 it brings joy
- In Ps. 17:7 it brings salvation
- In Ps. 18:35 it sustains us
- In Ps 20:6 it is victorious in power
- In Ps 21:8 it seizes the foe
- In Ps. 44: 13 it brings victory
- In Ps 89:13 it is filled with power
- In Ps 118: 16 it has done "mighty things"

James 1 instructs us to treat our trials as friends, because through them God is developing maturity in our lives. But we can also face our trials with confidence, knowing that the Heavenly Father is holding us by our right hand, walking beside us and acting on our behalf.

Psalm 98:1 says "Sing to the Lord a new song, for He has done marvelous things; his RIGHT HAND and His holy arm have worked salvation…" We can face not only our present circumstance but the future with boldness and without fear, knowing that with GOD holding our right hand there is absolutely no reason to be afraid.

THOUGHT: "Many Christians estimate difficulty in the light of their own resources, and thus they attempt very little and they always fail. All giants have been weak men who did great things for God because they reckoned on His power and presence to be with them". (Hudson Taylor)

40 - VISION

"Where there is no vision, the people perish " (Prov. 29:18 KJV)

J.C. Penney worked every day well into his 90's. One day he was brought some documents to sign. He looked at them, handed them to one of his administrators and said, "Please read these to me…I have lost my vision". Suddenly he stopped himself.
"WAIT!!" he exclaimed. "I have lost my EYESIGHT, I will NEVER lose my VISION!!!!"

Webster defines "vision" as "the act or power of imagination, unusual discernment or foresight". It is the ability to see what others can't see…the ability to see things not as they ARE, but as they COULD be. Every worship leader, every music ministry needs vision to flourish. Whether that includes a vision for staffing, facilities, ministry expansion, creative song selection and delivery, creative ways to accomplish outreach thru the music ministry, team structure, rehearsal planning, ministry growth, church growth….whatever area you might chose, "vision" is a critical ingredient for facing the future with optimism and creativity. It helps us "color outside the lines", helps us see the POTENTIAL…rather than the way things are right now.

David Jeremiah said "The only way the corporate Body of Christ will fulfill the mission Christ has given it is for individual Christians to have a vision for fulfilling that mission personally." It isn't just the responsibility of the worship leader to see the future through eyes of faith….it is the responsibility of every team member. What is YOUR vision for the future of your worship ministry?

THOUGHT: "When I think of vision, I have in mind the ability to see above and beyond the majority." (Charles Swindoll)

41 - UNITY IN LOVE

"Therefore, as God's chosen people, holy and dearly loved, clothe
yourselves with compassion, kindness, humility, gentleness and
patience. Bear with each other and forgive one another if any of you
has a grievance against someone. Forgive as the Lord forgave you.
And over all these virtues put on love, which binds them all together
in perfect unity." (Col. 3: 12-14 NIV)

The number one reason that missionaries leave their field of service
isn't lack of financial support, it isn't different, unusual food or living
arrangements, and it isn't being separated from family. The number one
reason missionaries come home from the field is....other missionaries!!
Col. 3 gives us a huge hint on working together as worship teams! We
are instructed to "put on" the garments of:

- **Compassion** (to be conscious of another's distress with a
  desire to alleviate it)
- **Kindness** (being warm hearted, considerate and forgiving
  of others)
- **Humility** (a modest opinion of one's own importance)
- **Gentleness** (acting in a mild, even-tempered manner)
- **Patience** (bearing annoyance or delay without anger)
- **Forgiveness** (the cancellation of a debt)
  and above all else,
- **LOVE,** which binds all the other garments together in
  perfect unity.

As worship teams we need to practice all of these characteristics,
because the one thing that will destroy a team member's desire to serve
above all other things is the attitude and behavior of fellow team
members. We can't preach unity from the platform unless we can live

it within our own team.

THOUGHT: I have never yet known the Spirit of God to work where the Lord's people were divided. (D.L. Moody)

42 - VOLUNTEER OR CALLED?

Rory Noland in his book, Heart of the Artist, (Zondervan, ISBN 0-310-22471-3) discusses the difference between those who volunteer out of obligation to serve in the church and those who feel called by God to serve. Noland says "that there is a deeper level of commitment, joy, and reward with those who know their calling is from God." He then lists differences between volunteers and those called of God:

> **1.** Volunteers see their involvement at church as community service, but people called of God see it as ministry.
>
> **2.** Volunteers whine about what it's going to cost to serve, but people called are committed to serving.
>
> **3.** Volunteers shrink back from resolving relational conflict, but people called of God seek to resolve relational conflict for the sake of unity in the church.
>
> **4.** Volunteers look upon rehearsal as another commitment they're obligated to fulfill, but people called of God look forward to rehearsal as another opportunity to be used by God.
>
> **5.** Volunteers do no outside practicing or preparation, but people who are called of God come to rehearsals and a performance as prepared as possible.
>
> **6.** Volunteers are not open to constructive criticism; they get defensive about it. But people called of God are grateful for feedback because they want to be the best they can be.
>
> **7.** Volunteers feel threatened by the talent of others, but people called of God praise Him for distributing gifts and talents as He chooses.
>
> **8.** Volunteers want to quit at the first sign of adversity or discouragement, but people called of God dig in and persevere.
>
> **9.** Volunteers find their main source of fulfillment in their talents and abilities, but people called of God know that being used of God is the most fulfilling thing you can do with your life.

10. Volunteers can't handle being put in situations in which they're going to be stretched, but people called of God respond to God's call with humble dependence on Him.

Noland summarizes by saying that God never intended ministry to be the responsibility of the chosen few who do 'full-time Christian work.' God has equipped all believers to do the work of ministry." (Ephesians 4:11-12) (taken from The Heart of the Artist, Pgs. 70-74)

43 - ONE ANOTHER

"This is my commandment, that you love one another as I have loved you." (John 15:12 NASB)

As a music ministry, we are a microcosm of the body of Christ, the church. The things that God instructed the church to do, we must …both as an example to the body of Christ and because God gave these instructions to show us how to live together in unity and purpose. Let's look at some of the "one another's" in scripture:

- Serve one another (John 13:14)
- Love one another (John 13:34, I Thess. 3:12)
- Be kindly affectionate to one another (Romans 12:10)
- Give preference to one another (Romans 12:10)
- Be of the same mind toward one another (Romans 12:16)
- Do not judge one another (Romans 14:13)
- Edify one another (Romans 14:19, I Thess. 5:11)
- Teach one another (Romans 15:14, Col. 3:16)
- Care for one another (I Cor. 12:25)
- Serve one another (Gal. 5:13)
- Bear one another's burdens (Gal. 6:2, Eph. 4:2)
- Be kind to one another (Eph. 4:32)
- Forgive one another (Eph. 4:32)
- Encourage one another (Eph. 5:19)
- Submit to one another (Eph. 5:21)
- Comfort one another (I Thess. 4:18)
- Pray for one another (James 5:16)

Do you see a pattern here? If we are to function effectively AS the body of Christ TO the body of Christ, we need to take to heart the "One Anothers" of God's Word...it isn't about ME, it is about US, as an example of unity and unconditional love.

THOUGHT: "Let no debt remain outstanding, except the continuing debt to love one another, for whoever loves others has fulfilled the law." (Rom. 13:8 NIV)

44 - JOB ONE

"And I, when I am lifted up from the earth, will draw all people to myself."   (John 12:32 NRSV)

In his great book on worship, entitled "One Thing Needful", Gary Mathena recounts this story: "A fire chief was training some new recruits, barking orders and making assignments. He assigned one man to polish the bell, another to tend the hoses, another to wash the truck, and another to cook. He continued until all the jobs were filled. After he made the assignments, he went back to the first man in line and asked, "Now what's your job?" the young rookie timidly replied "to polish the bell, Sir." Upon hearing that the chief put his nose against the nose of that young fireman and screamed "NO! That is not your job! Your job is putting out fires!!"

What is our "job one" as worship leaders? It is to point people toward Jesus Christ. As we lead worship songs that build up the body of Christ, we are pointing people to Jesus. As we sing songs about redemption, grace, mercy, and salvation, we are directing people to the Savior. As we share songs of encouragement, freedom, commitment and challenge, we are focusing on the work and person of Christ. No matter what the message in our times of worship, the OBJECT of our worship is Jesus, and HE is the focus of our corporate times of celebration.

Dr. Mathena goes on to say, "There are many necessary duties that must be attended to in the course of our ministry, many occupations that occupy our time, but we must never allow our occupations to take precedence over the vocation to which we have been called- the worship of God." As we lead in worship, remember that our FIRST priority is to lead people into the presence of Jesus...to direct people to the one answer for all of life's questions.

THOUGHT: "If Christianity is true, then every argument will, if pursued to the end, lead to Jesus." (John Mark Reynolds)

45 - MAKING A CLEAR PATH

"Therefore let us not judge one another anymore, but rather determine this--not to put an obstacle or a stumbling block in a brother's way."

(Romans 14:13 NASB)

Maria was interested in playing in orchestra, so Ruth and I took her and her fiancé to dinner. Knowing that she was from a religious group which adhered to a vegetarian viewpoint, Ruth and I ordered spaghetti with tomato sauce that evening, rather than risking offending her by eating a meat dish. Maria seemed genuinely grateful for our sensitivity, and went on to become one of our most valuable instrumentalists, growing in the Lord consistently as she sat under the teaching of our pastor week after week.

Paul's directive to the church at Rome has two sides: 1) Stop judging others in areas where their Christian liberty may not allow as much freedom as your liberty allows, and 2) don't offend that brother or sister by flaunting your spiritual maturity or your ability to partake of something which to them might be offensive. The guiding principle seems to be sensitivity motivated by love, rather than an attempt to "educate" a weaker brother or sister in how much freedom they COULD be experiencing.

When I was a young man, we had some guidelines in our home:
    NO movies
    NO TV on Sundays
    NO dancing, EVER

As a matter of fact, my father pulled me out of high school marching band because they did a cross-over dance step to the song "St Louis Blues"., and I remember him saying "No son of MINE is going to dance in marching band!!" now THAT is conservative! But with time, their perspectives matured and they loosened their grip on some of those guidelines. And that usually happens with Christian maturity...important things come more into focus, while peripheral issues become less critical.

Be patient with your brother and sister. Give them room to grow without forcing your freedom on them. And then, just as was the case with Maria, you will earn the right to minister to them more effectively.

THOUGHT: "Christianity resembles a narrow bridge spanning a place where two streams come together. One of those streams is crystal clear, but contains treacherous and deadly rapids; it symbolizes legalism--it appears to be a source of righteousness, but you can't stay afloat in it. Legalism will smash you on its rocks. The other stream is polluted libertinism-- if you fall into it, you will drown because of its filth. Therefore, the Christian must maintain his balance on the bridge between the treachery of legalism and the filth of libertinism". (John Macarthur)

46 - ON PSALM 150

We are all familiar with Psalm 150, and the fact that every family of instruments (brass, woodwinds, strings and percussion) is instructed to praise the Lord. But I love to look at cross references on passages like that to see "the rest of the story"! Here are 4 from the New American Standard Bible:

> 2 Samuel 6: 5- "Meanwhile, David and ALL the house of Israel were celebrating before the Lord with ALL KINDS of instruments made of fir wood, and with lyres, harps, tambourines, castanets and cymbals."

> I Chron. 13: 8 (a sister verse to 2 Sam. 6) David and ALL Israel were celebrating before God with ALL THEIR MIGHT, even with songs and with lyres, harps, tambourines, cymbals and with trumpets."

> Psalm 103:22- "Bless the Lord, ALL you works of His, in ALL places of His Dominion; Bless the Lord, O my soul!"

> Psalm 145:21- "My mouth will speak the praise of the Lord, and ALL flesh will bless His Holy name forever and ever."

WHAT DO WE SEE from these related passages? Here are a few insights:

1) EVERYONE was engaged in worship! There were no spectators or critics in this service, EVERYONE was involved!

2) They used EVERYTHING at their disposal to offer praise!

3) They were involved with EVERYTHING within them...they worshiped with ABANDON, holding NOTHING back!

4) Psalm 103 goes beyond the church, and instructs EVERYONE, EVERYWHERE to bring praise to the Almighty!

5) Psalm 145 instructs ALL flesh to praise him for EVER!

Do you see a pattern? Just as Christ has given EVERYTHING for us… So are we to respond to him with EVERYTHING we have! HE gives generously and unselfishly, and so should we!

THOUGHT: "To worship Him is to become more like Him and being formed in His image is all I desire. Worship Him with all you are." Glenna Dameron

47 - PROCESS vs. PRODUCT

"In whom the whole building, being fitted together, is growing into a

holy temple in the Lord, in whom you also are being built together

into a dwelling of God in the Spirit."

(Ephesians 2: 21-22 NASB)

God is in the process of bringing His children from a position of adolescence to one of maturity. This process takes time. Joseph Stowell, past President of Moody Bible Institute, writes this:

> "Some time ago, I was chatting with a man who consults with some of the largest U.S. companies about their quality control. Because ministry is a form of human quality control, I thought I'd ask him for some insights. He said, "In quality control, we are not concerned about the product." I was surprised. But then he went on to say, "We are concerned about the process. If the process is right, the product is guaranteed."

In worship ministry, the process is critical. While we have to be concerned about doing our very best every Sunday, we should be equally concerned with learning concepts each rehearsal that, once learned, will make it easier to participate with balance, blend, rhythmic accuracy, great intonation, etc, the **next** time we are on stage. As we build concept upon concept, we find the rehearsal process is much more effective, and is actually EASIER, because through the process we have learned new skills and ideas which we can utilize time after time.

A pencil (or RED pencil) is very important for an effective rehearsal, because once we have marked something, it should be correct from that point on. Then that part of the process is complete, and we can focus on learning NEW concepts and ideas which will make us all better individual musicians, and will improve the quality of the whole group.

The verse for today is a great illustration of the worship team, growing together, concept upon concept, into a mature, thriving organism designed to bring glory to God through excellence! As we develop the process, the product of excellence in our worship leadership will be a natural result.

THOUGHT: "Few things are impossible to diligence and skill. Great works are performed, not by strength, but perseverance." (Samuel Johnson)

48 - WORSHIP FROM THE HEART

"God is spirit, and those who worship Him must worship in spirit and truth." (John 4:24 NASB)

While in Kuala Lumpur, Malaysia, I visited the largest Hindu Shrine in the world...a golden statue that reaches some 120 feet in the air. It stands at the base of 272 steps, which lead to the caves. Inside the caves are literally hundreds of Hindu gods, and once a year a million Hindus throng to this sacred site to pay homage to some of their 330,000,000 wooden, stone and porcelain gods.

When Jesus met the woman at the well, and their conversation turned to worship, he made an interesting statement about worshipping in "spirit"....He was saying that worshipping God is all about RELATIONSHIP, and needed to take place with an attitude of wholehearted, genuine love. It is impossible to "love" an object that can't respond!

In the Bible we find many "expressions" of worship: kneeling (Ps.95:6, Eph. 3:14), clapping (Ps. 47:1, Ps. 98:8-9), lifting our hands (Ps. 134:1-2), and singing (Ps. 33:3) to name but a few. EACH of these postures or expressions assumes that the object of our worship can see, hear enjoy and appreciate our adoration! William Hendrickson writes that there are at least 60 references in the Bible to various postures of worship!!

Ray Steadman writes "We have personality because we are spirits dwelling in bodies. Our human spirit is designed to communicate and interrelate with the Spirit of God. That is what Jesus means when He says we must worship "in spirit". He is referring to our human spirit which is usually referred to in scripture as the "heart".

God designed us for relationship, and desires that our worship be motivated by a genuine, wholehearted love and adoration for His character, activity and provision. As we worship this week, let's be sure that our "hearts" are engaged....

THOUGHT: "When I worship I would rather my heart be without words than my words be without heart." Lamar Boschman

49 - TIMES OF TESTING (PART 1)

"Then Jesus was led by the Spirit into the wilderness to be tempted by

the Devil. After fasting forty days and forty nights, he was hungry.

The tempter came to him and said, 'If you are the Son of God, tell

these stones to become bread.' Jesus answered, 'It is written: Man

shall not live on bread alone, but on every word that comes from the

mouth of God.'" (Matthew 4: 1-4 NIV)

The word "tempted" can also be translated "tested"….and we are ALL tested from time to time...testing is actually a very helpful process, where we learn to lean on the Father, learn to use God's Word to stand firm and learn that God can give us the strength to resist thinking and behaving in ways that are in conflict with Godly values and theological truth.

In Matthew 4, Satan attacks Jesus by assuming that Jesus was filled with FEAR...in this case fear of going hungry, fear of not having enough strength, fear of not having his basic needs met. Jesus had just fasted for 40 days, and was hungry…so Satan attacked him where he was weakest and neediest! You and I face the same Satanic tactic, so we need to identify the source of our fears.
- Fear of loneliness
- Fear of lack of recognition
- Fear of having unmet needs
- Fear of rejection
- Fear of_____(YOU fill in the blank)

Jesus response was to TRUST THE FATHER. Whatever our fears, our Father is faithful and will provide. When we are faced with FEAR, the antidote is TRUST.

THOUGHT: "Fear is faithlessness" George McDonald

50-TIMES OF TESTING (PART 2)

"Then the devil took him to the holy city and had him stand on the
highest point of the temple. 'If you are the Son of God,' he said,
'throw yourself down. For it is written: He will command his angels
concerning you, and they will lift you up in their hands,
so that you will not strike your foot against a stone.' Jesus answered
him, It is also written: "Do not put the Lord your God to the test."
(Matt. 4: 5-7 NIV)

Satan not only attacks at our point of FEAR, but at our point of PRIDE.
Jesus could have said…. "Look at ME…I can FLY!!" or He could have
said "Isn't this why I came? To draw a crowd and prove my strength??"
but instead He said "I trust My Father's PLAN, and I trust His
TIMETABLE...I won't get ahead of either one." Where does our
inherent pride show up the most?

- I want to be first
- I want to be seen
- I want to be heard
- AHEAD OF YOU!!

Confidence is belief in oneself, Pride is comparative...I want to be
PRAISED, I want to be NOTICED, and to be praised or noticed I have
to be ahead of YOU. Pride says "I can do it", confidence says "GOD
can do it through me if He chooses." In other words, TRUST THE
FATHER! Instead of promoting ourselves, promote HIM, in every
aspect of our lives, and HE will gain the glory from our position in
ministry.

THOUGHT: "Pride gets no pleasure out of having something, only out
of having more of it than the next person." C.S. Lewis

"Again, the devil took him to a very high mountain and showed him
all the kingdoms of the world and their splendor. 'All this I will give
you," he said, 'if you will bow down and worship me.' Jesus said to
him, 'Away from me, Satan! For it is written: 'Worship the Lord your
God, and serve him only.' Then the devil left him, and angels came
and attended him." (Matt 4: 8-11 NIV)

In addition to using FEAR and PRIDE, Satan attacks through GREED.
Here Satan offers Jesus ALL the kingdoms of the world, in exchange
for worship, but Jesus focuses on the ONLY object worthy of worship,
and Satan finally left him alone. Where do we fall prey to greed in our
lives?

-   I have to work longer hours...I can't come to choir or
    orchestra rehearsal

-   I can't have a quiet time this morning, I have to be at
    work early so I can make more sales

-   I can't give any extra to the church, I have been saving
    for a really nice vacation...

Greed is an obsession with accumulating more than one NEEDS or
DESERVES....and Satan loves to use this tactic to distract us from
sacrificing...ANYTHING. It is important to provide for ones' family,
it ISNT important to have more stuff than the neighbor has! Greed
stands in the way of priorities, and causes us to make REALLY bad
decisions. Jesus' response to greed?? TRUST THE FATHER. He
knows how much I need, and will provide it in His time...so I can
clearly keep my focus on my priorities without worrying about
gathering MORE. Don't give in to FEAR, or to PRIDE or to GREED,
but instead, TRUST THE FATHER, "and all these things will be added
unto you." (Matt. 6:33)

THOUGHT: As long as you want anything very much, especially more than you want God, it is an idol." A.B. Simpson

The Gospel Hat

Just before we left on a mission trip to San Salvadore, El Salvadore, we were warned that it would be a good idea to take a broad brimmed hat....the sun was hot and we would be outdoors, a lot. So I bought a straw hat with a green visor in the bill, and was very glad I had made the purchase.

About the third day of the trip, I met a young man named Danny....we quickly became friends. He introduced me to his family and his church friends, and went with us for the rest of the week as we went door to door sharing Christ. He soon dubbed my straw hat "the gospel hat", and every day he would brag on the "gospel hat." On our final day there, I gave Danny "the gospel hat". It was as though I had given him a hundred dollar bill - he danced and pranced, showed it off to his family, clutched it to his chest and wore it proudly. Several days after our return to the States, I received a letter from Danny, and he once again thanked me profusely for "the gospel hat." It doesn't take a lot to build a relationship...to win someone's trust and to be a friend. It could take something as simple as a "gospel hat". What do YOU have that could be shared in order to build a relationship? Your friendships will build bridges to the Kingdom...look for opportunities to be a friend.

A Coke for Jesus

A group of us took instrumentalists to Cuba to play concerts, and to teach at a seminary and at instrumental conferences. While I was waiting for our seminary concert to begin, I walked a block to a little soft drink stand on the corner. There a young man named Jose struck up a conversation...I soon discovered that he was a high school student, and that he really wanted to talk with me so he could practice speaking English! We had a great chat, and then it was about time for the concert. I invited Jose to come hear our group, and he excitedly said that he would come. During the second song I noticed Jose and a young lady come in the back door and take a seat about half way down the auditorium. After the concert, Jose and his sister both accepted

Christ….all because a young man wanted to practice his English. What do YOU have that can be used to build a Kingdom bridge? It could be something as simple as the ability to speak your native language!

Uncle John

We were teaching classes at a University in Pristina, Kosovo. The students were open, asked honest, thoughtful questions, and listened intently to the various team teachers as they discussed business ethics, evolution, writing, and a variety of other pertinent topics. During a break, two young students came up to us and began a conversation. Both spoke fluent Albanian, English and Spanish…they said they had learned Spanish by watching Spanish soap operas!! They soon dubbed me "Uncle John", a term of respect due to our age differences. As the week progressed we had many opportunities to share with these two students, and when we returned to the States we maintained a correspondence, giving us the privilege of sharing Christ with both of them.

God doesn't need our "ability" as much as He desires our "availability". As an elderly saint told evangelist Leo Humphries," Make yourself available to God to be used, and he will wear you out"!!!!

53 - CHRISTMAS LIGHTS

"I am the Lord's servant," Mary answered. "May your word to me be fulfilled." (Luke 1:38 NIV)

Derrick Johnson, in his book "The Wonder of Christmas" recounts the story of 10 year old David Johnathan Sturgeon of Denver. The year…1918, and young David is desperately ill. His father operates an electrical business, and to cheer him up puts a small lit evergreen in David's room. David looks out the window, points at the big evergreen tree on the lawn and exclaims "Oh, Daddy, please put some lights on that tree too! It would look wonderful!"

David's father DID put lights on the outdoor tree, and soon the neighbors caught the vision for the beauty, and before long all of Denver was beautifully lit for Christmas!

Imagine the fear and awe Mary must have felt when the angel announces to this young teenage girl that she will give birth to a very special baby, without ever having been with a man! Imagine what JOSEPH felt when He learned of the situation! But Mary's response is indicative of what it takes to "light" our worlds for Christ…she replied "I am the Lord's servant". A servant spirit is contagious…once we see it modeled it and lived out before us, it becomes much easier to live the sacrificial life of a humble servant.

Here is one more thought from Luke 1…Mary wonders out loud how God could have chosen HER, and so the angel Gabriel gives her the details of what will happen, and tells Mary that even her cousin Elizabeth is pregnant in her old age. Then the angel makes a statement that we should each memorize:" For no word from God will ever fail!!" (NIV) other versions put it this way: "For NOTHING will be impossible with God!" (HCSB) This Christmas season, don't analyze YOUR capabilities, or YOUR wisdom, but remember that NOTHING is impossible with God. Mary modeled servant faith, and her example became a light to the world. God will use YOU as well, as you yield it ALL to Him.

No one has **greater love** than this, that someone would lay down his

life for his friends.   (John 15:13-HCSB)

Nate attended Yale College with his best friend Ben, and graduated at the age of 18 to become a teacher. Two years later Nate received this note from his friend Ben, "Was I in your condition, I think the more extensive service would be my choice. Our Holy religion, the honor of our God, a glorious country, and a happy constitution is what we have to defend." So Nate signed up...as a first lieutenant in the 7th Connecticut regiment.

Within several months, General George Washington asked for a volunteer to go behind enemy lines to determine the location of the next British invasion of Manhattan Island. Nate was the only volunteer. Dressed as a Dutch schoolmaster he made it behind enemy lines, discovered the necessary information and was headed back to safety when he was apprehended, admitted to being a spy, and was sentenced to death. He requested a Bible...the request was denied...he requested a clergyman, that request was denied as well. He wrote several letters to family which were confiscated and destroyed so his friends and relatives would not know of his resolute commitment to his fledgling country, and the next morning he was hanged as a spy. History remembers him for these words, spoken by Nathan Hale from the gallows," I only regret that I have but one life to lose for my country."

Anything worth living for is worth dying for. The Civil War cost some 620,000 lives...In WW II over 920,000 Americans sacrificed their lives, and over 58,000 Americans died in the Vietnam conflict. According to Christian historian Mark Moore, some 163,000 Christians die every year for their faith. (www.markmoore.org) As believers we will be called on to not only PREACH courage, but to LIVE it! My prayer for those of us who sing, play and preach from the pulpit is that we will willingly say, "I only regret that I have but one life to lose...."

Made in the USA
Middletown, DE
21 January 2020

83528232R00066